The Legend of Robin Hood

A legend from England

Michaela Morgan

Illustrated by
Mark Beech

CONTENTS

OXFORD
UNIVERSITY PRESS

Dear Reader,

There are lots of exciting Robin Hood stories. Some are very, very old and some are very new.

You might have seen Robin Hood stories on television, in film and in cartoons, but once upon a time people used to just tell or sing the stories to each other.

We know most of our Robin Hood stories because they were passed on in songs or 'ballads'. The story I tell in this book was once one of these ballads.

I hope you enjoy it!

Michaela Morgan

Chapter 1
Robin

Robin was running, running, running for his life. Behind him a gang of burly men shouted.

Get him!

Catch him!

Cut off his ears!

Robin glanced back. The soldiers were getting closer! They were going to catch him.

But Robin was a quick thinker. He saw a clump of bushes and quick as a wink he leapt into it. He lay safely hidden in the leafy damp as the soldiers pounded by.

Robin lay still as a stone, breathing as quietly as he could. 'Safe at last!' he thought.

It was then he saw that the leaves and bushes all around him were moving ... they were moving towards him!

Were the trees really coming to life? No!
It was a group of shabby men. They were
muddy and dirty. Some of them had leaves
and twigs in their clothes and hair.

'Who are you?' they asked.

Chapter 2
Outlaws

'I am Robin of Loxley Hall but ...' Robin's voice shook. 'The Sheriff took my home and now my family are all ...'

'We understand, lad,' said one of the men.

'We've lost our families and homes too. Now we live like wild animals in these woods. The Sheriff's men call us outlaws and try to hunt us down – but they can't find us in here. You can join us. You'll be safe from the soldiers in the woods.'

The next morning Robin woke up. It
hadn't been easy to get to sleep on the cold,
hard ground.

During the night it had rained. Robin and
all the outlaws were wet, freezing and very,
very, VERY hungry.

Robin had an idea. He had one *great* skill that could help these men.

He took his bow and arrow and went off hunting ...

... and soon he was back with plenty of meat.

'Build a big fire,' he laughed. 'Let's get cooking!'

Soon, the men were warm, well fed and happy. One of the band spoke up. 'I think Robin should be our leader.'

The others agreed. Robin grinned. He had found a new home and family.

Chapter 3
The camp

As the days passed, Robin organised
the men.

Winter was coming so they built huts.

They camouflaged the huts with leaves
and twigs.

Inside, they used heaps of leaves to make
soft beds.

Robin made a new outfit for himself. It had a hood of green that he could pull over his head when he needed to hide among the bushes.

He gave himself a new name. 'I am no longer Robin of Loxley,' he said. 'From now on, I am Robin Hood.'

Let the adventures begin!

Robin trained the band.

He taught them how to make a bow and arrow.

He taught them how to *use* a bow and arrow.

They learnt how to climb and move quickly through the forest.

They learnt how to find their own food.

But most importantly, Robin taught them
to help the poor and people in need.

As the days went by, Robin saw that some of the men were becoming good archers.

And some were not!

Robin made a decision.

I'll give each of you a special job to suit your talents!

So, some became archers.

Some became lookouts.

Some became cooks.

Some became hunters.

Some built the huts.

And then there was Allan ...
Allan did not like fighting.

He was a terrible cook.

And the huts he built ...

... fell down.

'What are you good at?' Robin asked him.

'I am good at telling stories and making music. Oh, and I'm good at singing songs!' said Allan.

'Then you shall be our minstrel!' said Robin.

Allan told tales to keep the men cheerful. He sang songs all about Robin Hood and his Merry Men. He sang his songs wherever he went – in market squares, at festivals and at fairs.

Soon, everyone had heard about Robin Hood. More and more people came to join his band. They all wanted to help the poor and to fight the wicked Sheriff and his soldiers.

21

Chapter 4
The mysterious boy

One night, Robin was on lookout when he saw a boy coming through the woods. Robin jumped out. Immediately the boy pulled out his sword and started to fight.

It was a fierce fight but a fast one. Robin was an expert with a sword and much bigger than the boy.

When he had won, Robin stepped out of
the shadows and into the moonlight.

'You fight bravely,' said Robin.
'Would you like to join us and fight the
wicked Sheriff?'

Then, to Robin's surprise, the boy
burst into tears.

'I thought *you* were one of the Sheriff's men,' the boy sobbed. Then Robin saw that he had made a mistake. It wasn't a boy. It was a girl!

'My name is Marion,' said the girl. 'The Sheriff and his men have taken my home. He locked my parents up. He locked me up too but I took these clothes and ran away to get help. He wants me to marry one of his men.'

Chapter 5
To the rescue!

Robin called for his band of men and they set off to rescue Marion's home and family.

When they arrived at Marion's castle it was still dark.

'I'll show you a secret way in,' she whispered.

She led them in and put on a dress. 'They will be coming for me soon,' she said. 'It's almost daylight.'

Morning came and in marched the Sheriff.

'Well Marion, I hope a long night alone in the dark has helped you learn your lesson. It's time for you to marry my fine friend! You can't fight us.'

'Yes I can!' shouted Marion.

'You and whose army?' mocked the Sheriff.

'This army!' said Marion as one by one the Merry Men appeared.

They came from behind the curtains ...

from under the bed ...

from out of the shadows.

One by one
they stepped
out and drew
their swords.

The Sheriff took one look and turned and ran down the stairs, out of the castle and across the fields. Robin's men chased him.

'Catch him! Cut off his ears!' shouted Robin. But he was joking. He just wanted the Sheriff to know what it was like to be chased and frightened.

Marion hugged and kissed her parents. '*My* family and home are safe now!' she smiled. But other people needed help too. She looked at Robin. 'Let me join the band.'

'Well ...' said Robin. 'You are brave. You can use a sword ... and you can use your head, so I say ...

... yes, you can join us!'

Everyone cheered. Allan sang a song.

Our band is made of merry men
And merry maids as well,
We fight for good with Robin Hood
And have fine tales to tell!
We help the poor and needy,
We fight the bullies and the greedy,
We'll fight for good with Robin Hood
And have fine tales to tell!